This Gratitude Journal Belongs to

SVSHARE PRESS

Copyright ©2020, SVShare Press. All rights reserved.

You are amazing

As a teacher, you touch lives every day and the positive effects ripple out endlessly!

Practicing gratitude daily will not only help you be the best teacher you can be: it will also help you be the happiest, healthiest, most amazing all-around person you *deserve* to be.

The science on gratitude is all good. Simply thinking about the good things in your life, whether big or small, for even just a few minutes a day, works wonders!

You will increase your happiness, your ability to face challenges, and your positive influence on students and their families, coworkers, friends, loved ones and others.

This 2-Minute Gratitude Journal for Teachers, complete with inspirational quotes, will help you enjoy all the benefits of gratitude in just minutes a day.

Have a grateful day!

My Gratitude Journal

You help your students dream bigger and do more, even when they are not in your classroom.

I am thankful for... Date

_____
_____
_____

I am thankful for... Date

_____
_____
_____

I am thankful for... Date

_____
_____
_____

I am thankful for...   Date

_____
_____
_____

I am thankful for...   Date

_____
_____
_____

I am thankful for...   Date

_____
_____
_____

I am thankful for...   Date

_____
_____
_____

Who showed gratitude for me this week

_____

My Gratitude Journal

Teaching is heart work.

I am thankful for...   Date
_____
_____
_____

I am thankful for...   Date
_____
_____
_____

I am thankful for...   Date
_____
_____
_____

I am thankful for... Date

_____
_____

I am thankful for... Date

_____
_____

I am thankful for... Date

_____
_____

I am thankful for... Date

_____
_____

Who showed gratitude for me this week

_____

My GRatitude Journal

Think of practicing gratitude as using a yellow highlighter on your life.

I am thankful for...   Date
_____
_____
_____

I am thankful for...   Date
_____
_____
_____

I am thankful for...   Date
_____
_____
_____

I am thankful for...	Date

_____
_____

I am thankful for...	Date

_____
_____

I am thankful for...	Date

_____
_____

I am thankful for...	Date

_____
_____

Who showed gratitude for me this week

_____

My Gratitude Journal

Treat yourself like you would treat others. With kindness.

I am thankful for...   Date
_____
_____
_____

I am thankful for...   Date
_____
_____
_____

I am thankful for...   Date
_____
_____
_____

I am thankful for...						Date

_____
_____

I am thankful for...						Date

_____
_____

I am thankful for...						Date

_____
_____

I am thankful for...						Date

_____
_____

Who showed gratitude for me this week

_____

My Gratitude Journal

Showing your students that you're still a curious student inspires them more than appearing to have all the answers.

I am thankful for...　　　Date

_____
_____

I am thankful for...　　　Date

_____
_____

I am thankful for...　　　Date

_____
_____

I am thankful for...   Date

_____
_____

I am thankful for...   Date

_____
_____

I am thankful for...   Date

_____
_____

I am thankful for...   Date

_____
_____

Who showed gratitude for me this week

_____

My Gratitude Journal

May smiles be the most contagious thing in your class today.

I am thankful for...		Date

_____
_____
_____

I am thankful for...		Date

_____
_____
_____

I am thankful for...		Date

_____
_____
_____

I am thankful for...　　　　Date

_____
_____

I am thankful for...　　　　Date

_____
_____

I am thankful for...　　　　Date

_____
_____

I am thankful for...　　　　Date

_____
_____

Who showed gratitude for me this week

_____

My Gratitude Journal

Aim for progress. Not perfection.

I am thankful for...　　　　Date

_____
_____
_____

I am thankful for...　　　　Date

_____
_____
_____

I am thankful for...　　　　Date

_____
_____
_____

I am thankful for... Date

_____
_____
_____

I am thankful for... Date

_____
_____
_____

I am thankful for... Date

_____
_____
_____

I am thankful for... Date

_____
_____
_____

Who showed gratitude for me this week

_____

My Gratitude Journal

To teach is to touch a life forever.

♡ I am thankful for...   Date

_____
_____

✏ I am thankful for...   Date

_____
_____

♡ I am thankful for...   Date

_____
_____

I am thankful for...   Date

_____
_____

I am thankful for...   Date

_____
_____

I am thankful for...   Date

_____
_____

I am thankful for...   Date

_____
_____

Who showed gratitude for me this week

_____

My Gratitude Journal

Teachers who love teaching teach students to love learning.

♡ I am thankful for...					Date

_____
_____
_____

✏️ I am thankful for...					Date

_____
_____
_____

♡ I am thankful for...					Date

_____
_____
_____

I am thankful for...   Date

_____
_____
_____

I am thankful for...   Date

_____
_____
_____

I am thankful for...   Date

_____
_____
_____

I am thankful for...   Date

_____
_____
_____

Who showed gratitude for me this week

_____

My Gratitude Journal

Don't limit your challenges.
Challenge your limits.

I am thankful for...   Date

_____
_____
_____

I am thankful for...   Date

_____
_____
_____

I am thankful for...   Date

_____
_____
_____

I am thankful for... Date

_____
_____
_____

I am thankful for... Date

_____
_____
_____

I am thankful for... Date

_____
_____
_____

I am thankful for... Date

_____
_____
_____

Who showed gratitude for me this week

_____

My Gratitude Journal

Be the teacher you needed when you were a student.

I am thankful for...   Date
_____
_____
_____

I am thankful for...   Date
_____
_____
_____

I am thankful for...   Date
_____
_____
_____

I am thankful for...   Date

_____
_____
_____

I am thankful for...   Date

_____
_____
_____

I am thankful for...   Date

_____
_____
_____

I am thankful for...   Date

_____
_____
_____

Who showed gratitude for me this week

_____

My Gratitude Journal

> The positive difference you are making in the lives of your students ripples out to countless others.

I am thankful for...   **Date**

_____
_____
_____

I am thankful for...   **Date**

_____
_____
_____

I am thankful for...   **Date**

_____
_____
_____

I am thankful for...					Date

_____
_____

I am thankful for...					Date

_____
_____

I am thankful for...					Date

_____
_____

I am thankful for...					Date

_____
_____

Who showed gratitude for me this week

_____

My Gratitude Journal

The power of self-talk is wonderful. As long as you talk to yourself as a friend.

I am thankful for...   Date

_____
_____
_____

I am thankful for...   Date

_____
_____
_____

I am thankful for...   Date

_____
_____
_____

I am thankful for...		Date

_____
_____

I am thankful for...		Date

_____
_____

I am thankful for...		Date

_____
_____

I am thankful for...		Date

_____
_____

Who showed gratitude for me this week

_____

My Gratitude Journal

> Difficult roads often lead to beautiful destinations.

I am thankful for...   Date

_____
_____
_____

I am thankful for...   Date

_____
_____
_____

I am thankful for...   Date

_____
_____
_____

I am thankful for...   Date

_____
_____
_____

I am thankful for...   Date

_____
_____
_____

I am thankful for...   Date

_____
_____
_____

I am thankful for...   Date

_____
_____
_____

Who showed gratitude for me this week

_____

My Gratitude Journal

Make today so awesome that yesterday gets jealous.

I am thankful for...   Date

_____
_____
_____

I am thankful for...   Date

_____
_____
_____

I am thankful for...   Date

_____
_____
_____

I am thankful for...   Date

_____
_____

I am thankful for...   Date

_____
_____

I am thankful for...   Date

_____
_____

I am thankful for...   Date

_____
_____

Who showed gratitude for me this week

_____

My Gratitude Journal

What doesn't kill you makes you stronger. Bet you're pretty swole by now.

I am thankful for...   Date

_____
_____

I am thankful for...   Date

_____
_____

I am thankful for...   Date

_____
_____

I am thankful for...		Date

_____
_____

I am thankful for...		Date

_____
_____

I am thankful for...		Date

_____
_____

I am thankful for...		Date

_____
_____

Who showed gratitude for me this week

_____

My Gratitude Journal

The more grateful you are, the more beauty you will see.

I am thankful for...   Date

_____
_____

I am thankful for...   Date

_____
_____

I am thankful for...   Date

_____
_____

I am thankful for...   Date

_____
_____
_____

I am thankful for...   Date

_____
_____
_____

I am thankful for...   Date

_____
_____
_____

I am thankful for...   Date

_____
_____
_____

Who showed gratitude for me this week

_____

My Gratitude Journal

> Being grateful doesn't mean that everything is fantastic. It just means you can accept it as a gift.

I am thankful for...   **Date**

_____
_____
_____

I am thankful for...   **Date**

_____
_____
_____

I am thankful for...   **Date**

_____
_____
_____

I am thankful for...　　　Date

_____
_____

I am thankful for...　　　Date

_____
_____

I am thankful for...　　　Date

_____
_____

I am thankful for...　　　Date

_____
_____

Who showed gratitude for me this week

_____

My Gratitude Journal

Practicing gratitude does not make life perfect. But it will make a life that is more perfect for YOU.

I am thankful for...　　　　Date

_____
_____
_____

I am thankful for...　　　　Date

_____
_____
_____

I am thankful for...　　　　Date

_____
_____
_____

I am thankful for...   Date

_____
_____

I am thankful for...   Date

_____
_____

I am thankful for...   Date

_____
_____

I am thankful for...   Date

_____
_____

Who showed gratitude for me this week

_____

My Gratitude Journal

> To make a positive difference in someone's life, you do not have to be a genius or perfect. You just have to care.

I am thankful for...   Date

_____
_____

I am thankful for...   Date

_____
_____

I am thankful for...   Date

_____
_____

I am thankful for...   Date

_____
_____
_____

I am thankful for...   Date

_____
_____
_____

I am thankful for...   Date

_____
_____
_____

I am thankful for...   Date

_____
_____
_____

Who showed gratitude for me this week

_____

My Gratitude Journal

A teacher is a star who teachers others how to shine.

I am thankful for...					Date

_____
_____
_____

I am thankful for...					Date

_____
_____
_____

I am thankful for...					Date

_____
_____
_____

I am thankful for...					Date

_____
_____
_____

I am thankful for...					Date

_____
_____
_____

I am thankful for...					Date

_____
_____
_____

I am thankful for...					Date

_____
_____
_____

Who showed gratitude for me this week

_____

My Gratitude Journal

A teacher's days are long, but the years are short.

I am thankful for...   Date

_____
_____

I am thankful for...   Date

_____
_____

I am thankful for...   Date

_____
_____

I am thankful for...					Date

_____
_____

I am thankful for...					Date

_____
_____

I am thankful for...					Date

_____
_____

I am thankful for...					Date

_____
_____

Who showed gratitude for me this week

_____

My Gratitude Journal

> If you're able to believe in the Tooth Fairy for years, you can definitely believe in yourself for the day.

I am thankful for...　　　　Date

_____
_____
_____

I am thankful for...　　　　Date

_____
_____
_____

I am thankful for...　　　　Date

_____
_____
_____

I am thankful for...   Date

_____
_____
_____

I am thankful for...   Date

_____
_____
_____

I am thankful for...   Date

_____
_____
_____

I am thankful for...   Date

_____
_____
_____

Who showed gratitude for me this week

_____

My Gratitude Journal

> People who wonder if the glass is half empty or half full are missing the point: The glass can be refilled.

I am thankful for...   Date

_____
_____
_____

I am thankful for...   Date

_____
_____
_____

I am thankful for...   Date

_____
_____
_____

I am thankful for...   Date

_____
_____

I am thankful for...   Date

_____
_____

I am thankful for...   Date

_____
_____

I am thankful for...   Date

_____
_____

Who showed gratitude for me this week

_____

My Gratitude Journal

May your coffee be hot and strong and your students cooperative and curious.

I am thankful for...		Date

_____
_____

I am thankful for...		Date

_____
_____

I am thankful for...		Date

_____
_____

I am thankful for...   Date

_____
_____

I am thankful for...   Date

_____
_____

I am thankful for...   Date

_____
_____

I am thankful for...   Date

_____
_____

Who showed gratitude for me this week

_____

My Gratitude Journal

> There will be good days and bad days and you will learn priceless lessons from both.

I am thankful for...   Date

_____
_____
_____

I am thankful for...   Date

_____
_____
_____

I am thankful for...   Date

_____
_____
_____

I am thankful for...   Date

_____
_____

I am thankful for...   Date

_____
_____

I am thankful for...   Date

_____
_____

I am thankful for...   Date

_____
_____

Who showed gratitude for me this week

_____

My Gratitude Journal

Thank YOU for teaching
our future leaders.

I am thankful for...   Date

_____
_____
_____

I am thankful for...   Date

_____
_____
_____

I am thankful for...   Date

_____
_____
_____

I am thankful for...   Date

_____
_____
_____

I am thankful for...   Date

_____
_____
_____

I am thankful for...   Date

_____
_____
_____

I am thankful for...   Date

_____
_____
_____

Who showed gratitude for me this week

_____

My Gratitude Journal

Keep calm and pretend it's in the lesson plan.

I am thankful for...   Date

_____
_____
_____

I am thankful for...   Date

_____
_____
_____

I am thankful for...   Date

_____
_____
_____

I am thankful for...　　　Date

_____
_____

I am thankful for...　　　Date

_____
_____

I am thankful for...　　　Date

_____
_____

I am thankful for...　　　Date

_____
_____

Who showed gratitude for me this week

_____

My Gratitude Journal

_____

Show your students how
to throw kindness around
like it's confetti.

I am thankful for...   **Date**

_____
_____
_____

I am thankful for...   **Date**

_____
_____
_____

I am thankful for...   **Date**

_____
_____
_____

I am thankful for...　　　Date

_____
_____

I am thankful for...　　　Date

_____
_____

I am thankful for...　　　Date

_____
_____

I am thankful for...　　　Date

_____
_____

Who showed gratitude for me this week

_____

My Gratitude Journal

Today, mistakes will be made, lessons will be learned, and laughter will be shared.

I am thankful for...　　　　Date

_____
_____
_____

I am thankful for...　　　　Date

_____
_____
_____

I am thankful for...　　　　Date

_____
_____
_____

I am thankful for...   Date

_____
_____
_____

I am thankful for...   Date

_____
_____
_____

I am thankful for...   Date

_____
_____
_____

I am thankful for...   Date

_____
_____
_____

Who showed gratitude for me this week

_____

My Gratitude Journal

> If you find yourself digging deeper and deeper for patience and understanding, just remember that each bit of kindness will bring you the good karma you deserve.

I am thankful for...   Date

_____
_____
_____

I am thankful for...   Date

_____
_____
_____

I am thankful for...   Date

_____
_____
_____

I am thankful for... Date

_____
_____
_____

I am thankful for... Date

_____
_____
_____

I am thankful for... Date

_____
_____
_____

I am thankful for... Date

_____
_____
_____

Who showed gratitude for me this week

_____

My Gratitude Journal

Struggle is good. It's when the brain is growing most.

I am thankful for...   Date

_____
_____

I am thankful for...   Date

_____
_____

I am thankful for...   Date

_____
_____

I am thankful for...   Date

_____
_____

I am thankful for...   Date

_____
_____

I am thankful for...   Date

_____
_____

I am thankful for...   Date

_____
_____

Who showed gratitude for me this week

_____

My Gratitude Journal

You are making a positive difference. Every. Single. Day.

I am thankful for...   Date

_____
_____
_____

I am thankful for...   Date

_____
_____
_____

I am thankful for...   Date

_____
_____
_____

I am thankful for...   Date

_____
_____

I am thankful for...   Date

_____
_____

I am thankful for...   Date

_____
_____

I am thankful for...   Date

_____
_____

Who showed gratitude for me this week

_____

My Gratitude Journal

Gratitude turns what we have into "enough."

♡ I am thankful for...   Date

_____
_____
_____

✏ I am thankful for...   Date

_____
_____
_____

♡ I am thankful for...   Date

_____
_____
_____

I am thankful for...		Date
_____
_____

I am thankful for...		Date
_____
_____

I am thankful for...		Date
_____
_____

I am thankful for...		Date
_____
_____

Who showed gratitude for me this week

_____

My Gratitude Journal

A person who is not thankful for what they have is unlikely to be thankful for what they get.

I am thankful for...   Date
_____
_____
_____

I am thankful for...   Date
_____
_____
_____

I am thankful for...   Date
_____
_____
_____

I am thankful for...   Date

_____
_____

I am thankful for...   Date

_____
_____

I am thankful for...   Date

_____
_____

I am thankful for...   Date

_____
_____

Who showed gratitude for me this week

_____

My Gratitude Journal

> Be grateful for the small things in life, because you may look back and realize they were the big things.

I am thankful for...   Date

_____
_____
_____

I am thankful for...   Date

_____
_____
_____

I am thankful for...   Date

_____
_____
_____

I am thankful for...   Date

_____
_____

I am thankful for...   Date

_____
_____

I am thankful for...   Date

_____
_____

I am thankful for...   Date

_____
_____

Who showed gratitude for me this week

_____

My Gratitude Journal

> Never put the key to your happiness in someone else's pocket.

I am thankful for... **Date**

_____
_____
_____

I am thankful for... **Date**

_____
_____
_____

I am thankful for... **Date**

_____
_____
_____

I am thankful for...   Date

_____
_____
_____

I am thankful for...   Date

_____
_____
_____

I am thankful for...   Date

_____
_____
_____

I am thankful for...   Date

_____
_____
_____

Who showed gratitude for me this week

_____

My Gratitude Journal

> Teaching is the profession that teaches all other professions.

I am thankful for...   Date

_____
_____
_____

I am thankful for...   Date

_____
_____
_____

I am thankful for...   Date

_____
_____
_____

I am thankful for...   Date

_____
_____
_____

I am thankful for...   Date

_____
_____
_____

I am thankful for...   Date

_____
_____
_____

I am thankful for...   Date

_____
_____
_____

Who showed gratitude for me this week

_____

My Gratitude Journal

Sometimes those who
challenge you the most,
teach you the most.

I am thankful for...　　　　Date

_____
_____
_____

I am thankful for...　　　　Date

_____
_____
_____

I am thankful for...　　　　Date

_____
_____
_____

I am thankful for...   Date

_____
_____

I am thankful for...   Date

_____
_____

I am thankful for...   Date

_____
_____

I am thankful for...   Date

_____
_____

Who showed gratitude for me this week

_____

My Gratitude Journal

Mistakes are proof
that you are trying.

I am thankful for...   Date

_____
_____
_____

I am thankful for...   Date

_____
_____
_____

I am thankful for...   Date

_____
_____

I am thankful for...   Date

_____
_____

I am thankful for...   Date

_____
_____

I am thankful for...   Date

_____
_____

I am thankful for...   Date

_____
_____

Who showed gratitude for me this week

_____

My Gratitude Journal

> Don't let the perfect be the enemy of the good.

I am thankful for...   Date

_____
_____

I am thankful for...   Date

_____
_____
_____

I am thankful for...   Date

_____
_____
_____

I am thankful for...   Date

_____
_____

I am thankful for...   Date

_____
_____

I am thankful for...   Date

_____
_____

I am thankful for...   Date

_____
_____

Who showed gratitude for me this week

_____

My Gratitude Journal

> You can't serve others from an empty cup. So make sure to refill yours by doing things that make you smile.

♥ I am thankful for...   Date

_____
_____
_____

✏ I am thankful for...   Date

_____
_____
_____

♥ I am thankful for...   Date

_____
_____
_____

I am thankful for...   Date

_____
_____

I am thankful for...   Date

_____
_____

I am thankful for...   Date

_____
_____

I am thankful for...   Date

_____
_____

Who showed gratitude for me this week

_____

My Gratitude Journal

Showing students how you turn lemons into lemonade is a sweet victory for you both.

I am thankful for... Date
_____
_____
_____

I am thankful for... Date
_____
_____
_____

I am thankful for... Date
_____
_____
_____

I am thankful for...   Date

_____
_____
_____

I am thankful for...   Date

_____
_____
_____

I am thankful for...   Date

_____
_____
_____

I am thankful for...   Date

_____
_____
_____

Who showed gratitude for me this week

_____

My Gratitude Journal

Even super hero teachers
make super human mistakes.

♥ I am thankful for...   Date
_____
_____
_____

✏ I am thankful for...   Date
_____
_____
_____

♥ I am thankful for...   Date
_____
_____
_____

I am thankful for...   Date

_____
_____
_____

I am thankful for...   Date

_____
_____
_____

I am thankful for...   Date

_____
_____
_____

I am thankful for...   Date

_____
_____
_____

Who showed gratitude for me this week

_____

My Gratitude Journal

> The best teachers are those who tell you where to look but don't tell you what to see.

I am thankful for...   **Date**

_____
_____
_____

I am thankful for...   **Date**

_____
_____
_____

I am thankful for...   **Date**

_____
_____
_____

I am thankful for...   Date

_____
_____

I am thankful for...   Date

_____
_____

I am thankful for...   Date

_____
_____

I am thankful for...   Date

_____
_____

Who showed gratitude for me this week

_____

My Gratitude Journal

Kindness is free to give but priceless to receive.

I am thankful for... Date

_____
_____
_____

I am thankful for... Date

_____
_____
_____

I am thankful for... Date

_____
_____
_____

I am thankful for...   Date

_____
_____
_____

I am thankful for...   Date

_____
_____
_____

I am thankful for...   Date

_____
_____
_____

I am thankful for...   Date

_____
_____
_____

Who showed gratitude for me this week

_____

My Gratitude Journal

Be proud of the work you do,
the person you are and the
difference you make every day.

I am thankful for...   Date

_____
_____
_____

I am thankful for...   Date

_____
_____
_____

I am thankful for...   Date

_____
_____
_____

I am thankful for...		Date

_____
_____

I am thankful for...		Date

_____
_____

I am thankful for...		Date

_____
_____

I am thankful for...		Date

_____
_____

Who showed gratitude for me this week

_____

My Gratitude Journal

If a plan doesn't work, change the plan. Not the goal.

I am thankful for...　　　Date

_____
_____
_____

I am thankful for...　　　Date

_____
_____
_____

I am thankful for...　　　Date

_____
_____
_____

I am thankful for...   Date

_____
_____
_____

I am thankful for...   Date

_____
_____
_____

I am thankful for...   Date

_____
_____
_____

I am thankful for...   Date

_____
_____
_____

Who showed gratitude for me this week

_____

My Gratitude Journal

Your classroom is a place of learning, respect and love because you are in it.

I am thankful for...　　　　Date

_____
_____
_____

I am thankful for...　　　　Date

_____
_____
_____

I am thankful for...　　　　Date

_____
_____
_____

I am thankful for...　　　Date
_____
_____

I am thankful for...　　　Date
_____
_____

I am thankful for...　　　Date
_____
_____

I am thankful for...　　　Date
_____
_____

Who showed gratitude for me this week

_____

My Gratitude Journal

At this moment, imagine that someone else is giving thanks for you. Because they are.

I am thankful for...   Date

_____
_____
_____

I am thankful for...   Date

_____
_____
_____

I am thankful for...   Date

_____
_____
_____

I am thankful for... Date

_____
_____

I am thankful for... Date

_____
_____

I am thankful for... Date

_____
_____

I am thankful for... Date

_____
_____

Who showed gratitude for me this week

_____

My Gratitude Journal

Would rainbows inspire as much awe if they didn't follow stormy weather?

I am thankful for...   Date

_____
_____
_____

I am thankful for...   Date

_____
_____
_____

I am thankful for...   Date

_____
_____
_____

I am thankful for...   Date

_____
_____
_____

I am thankful for...   Date

_____
_____
_____

I am thankful for...   Date

_____
_____
_____

I am thankful for...   Date

_____
_____
_____

Who showed gratitude for me this week

_____

My Gratitude Journal

> When you have an attitude of gratitude, it's like experiencing life in high definition — more color, more detail, more impact.

I am thankful for...   Date

_____
_____
_____

I am thankful for...   Date

_____
_____
_____

I am thankful for...   Date

_____
_____
_____

I am thankful for...   Date

_____
_____
_____

I am thankful for...   Date

_____
_____
_____

I am thankful for...   Date

_____
_____
_____

I am thankful for...   Date

_____
_____
_____

Who showed gratitude for me this week

_____

My Gratitude Journal

You are an educational rockstar!

I am thankful for...   Date

_____
_____

I am thankful for...   Date

_____
_____

I am thankful for...   Date

_____
_____

I am thankful for...   Date

_____
_____

I am thankful for...   Date

_____
_____

I am thankful for...   Date

_____
_____

I am thankful for...   Date

_____
_____

Who showed gratitude for me this week

_____

Your Thoughts About Practicing Gratitude

You have been giving thanks in your journal for big and small things on a daily basis. What effect do you think this practice has had on your life?

Notes

Notes

Notes

Notes

Notes

Notes

Made in the USA
Columbia, SC
12 June 2024

37011827R00065